Choose
Love

Choose Love

Nicola Davies
Petr Horáček

GRAFFEG

Choose Love
Published in Great Britain in 2022 by Graffeg Limited.

Written by Nicola Davies copyright © 2022. Illustrations by Petr Horáček copyright © 2022. Designed by Peter Gill and Joana Rodrigues, edited by Matthew Howard and Daniel Williams, produced by Graffeg copyright © 2022.

Graffeg Limited, 15 Neptune Court, Vanguard Way, Cardiff, CF24 5PJ, Wales, UK. Tel 01554 824000. www.graffeg.com.

Nicola Davies is hereby identified as the author of this work in accordance with section 77 of the Copyright, Designs and Patents Act 1988.

A CIP Catalogue record for this book is available from the British Library.

All rights reserved. No part of this publication may be reproduced, stored in a retrieval system or transmitted, in any form or by any means, electronic, mechanical, photocopying, recording or otherwise, without the prior permission of the publishers.

ISBN 9781802583779

1 2 3 4 5 6 7 8 9

Contents

Choose Love	5
Foreword by Onjali Raúf	6
DEPARTURE	**9**
THIS MOMENT	10
BEFORE WE LEFT	13
FIVE MINUTES	14
MATHEMATICS	17
ARRIVAL	**19**
SUPERMARKET FLOWERS	20
THE TRIALS	23
THE INTERVIEW	25
ARTIN'S VOYAGE	28
HEALING	**31**
HOPE	32
NOT LOST	35
SPIDERMAN	36
UNBROKEN	39
Notes	40
Choose Love Charity	42
Nicola Davies	44
Petr Horáček	46

Choose Love

Welcome the traveller from the distant land

With his unfamiliar face,

With her language you don't understand,

She is yourself,

He is your kin.

One day, you too will have to leave,

Without warning or goodbyes,

To travel to an unknown country.

So, choose love, now,

While you still can.

Foreword

There have been many moments in my life when I have been rendered utterly speechless by the happenings of the world. Most of these moments have revolved around bearing witness to acts of inhumanity, often spurred on by racisms so visceral it is unfathomable and designed to harm yet further an already deeply hurt group of human hearts.

Being interrogated at border controls about the tents, sleeping bags, toys and nappies my teams and I have packed to the rafters of our cars for awaiting refugees only to be grudgingly let through thanks to that tiny emblem of privilege that is the British passport leaves me speechless every time.

Seeing armed police sporting batons and rifles, ready to tear what a refugee family has away from them yet again, leaves me struggling to find even the most basic of words, as does having to read of yet another life gone, extinguished, wiped out in a race for survival – as if each one didn't matter and wasn't connected to, and loved by, another.

And as for the stories – histories told in real time by people surviving what most of us cannot even bear to think of – each and every story a refugee honours me with leaves me speechless and humbled in a million unending ways.

This 'crisis' we hear of, breaking through our news channels every so often, is not a refugee crisis. It is a crisis of man-made borders and decisions, all of which will have repercussions beyond our imaginings and upon generations to come.

The silence around it needs to be broken.

Not with sensational headlines, but words which convey truths. Real, humanising, humane truths, capable of dismantling the boogey monster of 'The Refugee' lurking in the minds of many who are lucky enough to be residing in a land (currently) safe from war, or climate change disasters occurring on a mass scale.

In this beautiful collection of poems, Nicola has gifted us those words – words sorely needed to bring truths to the fore and rehumanise those who have been dehumanised to the point of non-existence. Encapsulating the experiences of flight, survival, confusion and a search for answers, each of her poems, coupled with the innocence of Horáček's drawings, shines a light on real-time moments and histories unfolding all around us.

Each one has left me speechless once more, albeit this time in a state of perpetual hope for kinder, better worlds and words ahead...

Onjali Raúf

Departure

DEPARTURE

THIS MOMENT

Of course, you saw this moment coming:
It was in the space between the flags and placards
on the street, behind the camouflage of newsprint.
A distant megaphone announced it months ago,
The boarded windows and the bombs
confirmed its imminent arrival.

It was too big to understand,
yet somehow small enough to hide,
to fold between the wind-dried sheets,
stir back into the stew,
and slide underneath the bed.

It didn't stay where it was put.
And now it's on the doorstep,
shouting like a drunk:
This moment,
This moment,
This moment from which nothing will ever be the same.

BEFORE WE LEFT

For months we listened, huddled in the dark,
to Mother's words, like hail battering the roof:
"It is too dangerous.
It is too far.
It is too expensive.
It is too cold.
It is too lonely."
To Father's silence.

When at last his words came,
they lodged beneath our eyelids
the way sand does, rubbing, chaffing,
"There is no future here,
we have to leave."
We listened, huddled in the dark.
Afraid.

FIVE MINUTES

You've got five minutes, what will you choose
From all that you're about to lose?

You've got five minutes to fill your arms,
When the city shrieks with fire alarms.

You've got five minutes, what will you bring?
A hat? A coat? A wedding ring?

You've got five minutes, no time for pain,
Because bricks and mortar fall like rain.

You've got five minutes to save a life,
Your sleeping children, your brother's wife?

You've got five minutes to run, run, run,
While the sky burns up like a dying sun.

You've got five minutes to count the cost
Of the past and future you just lost.

MATHEMATICS

Two hundred on a tiny boat,
Forty drowned when it won't float.
Eight thousand in a camp for two,
Seventy sharing a portaloo.
Sixteen crammed in an isobox,
Thirty down with chicken pox.

No roof, no food, no clothes, no soap.
No home, no dignity, no hope.
Humans crammed on overload,
No surprise that they explode.
Rules are made with gun and knife,
And ten year olds take their own life.

Countless corpses in the sea,
This is the maths of misery.
A rising tide of pain and sorrow
And forty thousand more tomorrow.
This is the maths of misery.
It could be you, it could be me.

ARRIVAL

ARRIVAL

SUPERMARKET FLOWERS

Why is he here?

Listen and he'll tell you:

Because his land was stolen

by someone who could read and write.

Because his river was poisoned so no crops would grow.

Because his children starved.

Because he wants to ask you 'why',

why you bought that bunch of supermarket flowers

without knowing what the price was, or who paid it.

THE TRIALS

First the trial of escape:
leaping from the monster's mouth while its jaws snap;
fleeing with the flames and famine licking at your heels;
nights of terror wondering about the ones
you had to leave behind.

Then the trial of distance:
jolting in the back of stinking trucks with fifty others;
trying to keep your child warm in falling snow;
bleeding feet, nowhere to wash,
men screaming in languages you don't understand.

But now you have arrived, the worst trial:
waiting.
Waiting with no country, no place to go, no job to do,
while someone decides if what you've suffered is enough.

The Interview

Where you grew up, there was a calendar
with rural scenes above the aga.
You crossed off the days before your birthday.
You aren't supposed to use it as a password, but you do.
How can a person not know
the date that they were born on?
It makes you suspicious from the start.

At school, they tried to teach you French,
five years of study and ordering a coffee is beyond you.
If, as she claims, she never went to school,
how come she's fluent in three languages?
Who taught her? Why?

No one could say you're ignorant of trauma;
your husband buggered off without a warning
and left the bills unpaid.
You talked about it for a year without a breath.
But when you ask her why she left her homeland,
she's halting, tongue-tied.
It's obvious she's lying.

You can't imagine what she's been through,
you really can't:
the terror that has bitten to her bones,
the storm of grief and chaos that blew her to your desk.
Your little life's too narrow to let you understand
the meaning of asylum, and why she needs it.
You sigh, and stamp rejected on the forms.

The crucial moment for asylum seekers is the 'Substantive Interview', where the interviewee's account of their reasons for asylum seeking are rigorously tested and challenged. People wait for months and years for their interview, only to experience a gruelling ordeal which results in the rejection of their claim.

Artin's Voyage

We can't be sure which way he went,

Through the Southern Bight and over Dogger Bank

Into the Jutland current perhaps, then North to Karmoy,

Where a light easterly brought him in on New Year's Day.

No one knew him there, or guessed how far he'd come,

Six hundred miles is, after all,

A long way for a toddler,

All alone.

I think of him, at sea,

Floating in his small blue suit;

The weeks of autumn skies overhead,

The clouds, the sinking stars,

The swells pockmarked with rain.

At last, the retreating fingers of the tide

Leaving him to the arrival

That his parents never planned.

In memory of Artin Irannezhad, his parents, brother and sister, who drowned on 27th October 2020 during their third attempt to cross the Channel to the UK to seek asylum. Artin's body was found on New Year's Day 2021 on the coast of Norway.

HEALING

HEALING

HOPE

A bomb took his brother,
A sniper's bullet took his dad,
and when you asked about his mum and sister,
he just looked away.

So, when his was the only sunflower that
didn't come up,
I thought, jeez, the Universe really doesn't like this kid.
I didn't blame him when he threw the pot against
the wall.
But in the middle of the muddy impact zone
there was a speck of green;
a minute, fragile finger poking
from that skinny, stripy little seed.

He picked it up, refilled the pot,
replanted it with such tenderness,
then, for the first time, smiled.
I had to turn away to hide the tears
as a tiny shoot of hope stirred inside me, too.

NOT LOST

We had to walk and walk and walk.
Mum held my little sister and couldn't hold my hand.
She wrapped my fingers round the button on her coat,
"So you'll be safe," she said, "and won't be lost!"
I held on tight,
even on the boat.
Even when I fell asleep.

I held on to the button when they pulled me
from the sea.
I hold it still, on a string, next to my heart.
So I remember how Mum loved me
and that I'm not lost.

SPIDERMAN

Everyday, Spiderman winds string around the table legs,

Through the backs of chairs,

Over the blackboard.

Across, between, beneath, and back again.

He whispers to his web, like a nun with her rosary,

Repeating the stations of his journey:

The place names and the terrors;

The blood-splashed days;

The nights of sleepless cold;

The people he has lost,

Where and when and how.

We are all tangled in his timeline.

It threads around our ankles and our arms

And through our hair.

Only he can rescue us. This is the game:

Meticulously, he unwinds his string,

Spools back his story onto the bobbin of his soul.

Each time he gains a little power.

Each time he's closer to a superhero.

UNBROKEN

The china cup was my mother's,
The one small thing of beauty in her harsh life.
It held her smile, her hands as rough and gnarled as branches
With their tender touch.
I carried it across continents and oceans,
The one small thing of beauty in my lost life.
It held my endurance and my patience.

Today it broke.
I can no longer endure.
I can no longer be patient.
My rage consumes me,
For what is broken cannot be unbroken.
Our shattered past,
Our fractured future
are beyond mending.

My daughter takes the shards.
With her granny's tender touch,
she pieces them together.
Patient when it seems they do not fit.
Enduring when their edges cut her fingers.
She hands me back the cup, whole.
"Unbroken," she says.
"Unbroken!"

Notes

In 2016 I had been trying to write something about the humanitarian crisis caused by the war in Syria. I had got as far as making some notes, but then the UK government refused to help 3000 unaccompanied child refugees and I was galvanised into action by a mixture of utter fury and shame for the unwelcoming, selfish nation we seemed to have become. I wrote a picture book text called *The Day War Came*, from the perspective of a child who had lost everything, family, home, safety, education, and who found herself in a hut in a refugee camp. I finished the text in the morning and by mid afternoon it was on the *Guardian* website. The text features an empty chair as a symbol of welcome and I invited readers to submit their pictures of empty chairs as small acts of solidarity with those children. My dear friends Petr Horáček and Jackie Morris were the first to contribute and many others flooded in (you can still see them online). When the book was launched, we auctioned the pictures to raise funds for the incredible charity Help Refugees, who became Choose Love. It has now been published in languages around the world.

The poems in this book were born out of my association with Choose Love and with the charity Refugee Trauma Initiative. Through these organisations I learned about the real-life experience of people who are forced to leave behind their homes, lives and loved ones by the violence of war, famine or oppression, and of the remarkable professionals who help them. It is those true stories and those real people that I have tried to represent in this work. I offer these poems, in love and with respect, in the hope that readers will realise that nothing but circumstance separates any of us from the experience of being a refugee. Humanity faces an uncertain future, and there is only one choice that will get us through. We need to contemplate its deepest meaning and make it anew every day: Choose Love, choose love, every time.

Nicola Davies

When Nicola asked me to illustrate her book *Choose Love*, I was excited. I was excited to have the opportunity to work with Nicola again, but after reading the poems I worried if I was the right person to illustrate the book. The poems are stunning. The subject and the importance of this book gave me a big responsibility.

So, Nicola and I made a deal: I would paint pictures inspired by the beautiful poems, no discussions, no compromises, no editing, and if Nicola and the publisher liked the finished illustrations, we would publish it with my pictures.

My illustrations are not pretty. They are expressive and heavy with texture. Familiar shapes or a human silhouette sometimes come to the surface. The colour is sporadic, but it's noticeable in the layers of heavy, mostly grey paint. Colour seeps through the paint just as love and hope seeps through Nicola's poems.

Love and hope, the two most important things in our lives, because... what else?

Petr Horáček

Choose Love Charity

CHOOSE LOVE

Choose Love is pioneering a new movement in humanitarian aid which is flexible, transparent and accountable, providing refugees and displaced people with everything from lifesaving search and rescue boats to food and legal advice. They elevate the voices and visibility of refugees and galvanise public support for agile community organisations, offering vital support to refugees along migration routes globally.

Their passionate team is driving a fast-paced movement, raising millions to support refugees and encouraging others to put love into action around the world. Going where the need is greatest, they find the local organisations doing the most effective work and give them what they need to help people – whether that's funding, material aid or volunteers. With this model they've managed to reach over 3.5 million people through over 390 projects in 33 countries.

From critical medical care to blankets and water, the ways in which they can provide support in emergency situations are wide-ranging and essential. This includes rescuing people from distress at sea and providing emergency medical treatment in the Mediterranean, securing life-saving supplies when disaster strikes to keep people safe and protected from the elements in Lebanon, supplying equipment and medical provisions for the most vulnerable in Greece and helping to create safe spaces and facilitating essential services for women and young girls, who are often particularly vulnerable.

For people living in tents and makeshift shelters, often for years, Choose Love arrange for hygiene kits, hot food, firewood and assistance for unaccompanied children as well as ongoing support on the long road towards rebuilding their lives, with vital education, mental health support and legal aid helping build a new start and a brighter future.

Visit www.chooselove.org to find out more about donating, volunteering, fundraising and taking action and how you can contribute to Choose Love's far-reaching work to help others in need.

Nicola Davies

Nicola Davies trained as a zoologist and studied bats and whales in the wild before joining the BBC Natural History Unit as a researcher and presenter of programmes such as *The Really Wild Show*. She became a children's author when her own children were in school and has written more than 80 books for children, fiction, non-fiction and poetry. Her work has won awards around the world and been published in more than twelve different languages.

Although her work focuses mainly on the natural world, she has a strong interest in the welfare of children and has written books addressing issues such as grief, disability, bullying and children's rights. She has written two books about child refugees, *King of the Sky*, about the Italian diaspora in the depression of the 1920s, and *The Day War Came*, about a child fleeing war having lost all her family.

Some of her recent work with Graffeg includes poetry for adults and for children: *The Versatile Reptile* and *Invertebrates are Cool* are rhyming celebrations illustrated by Abbie Cameron of typically reviled sections of the animal kingdom, and *This is How the Change Begins* is a collection of poems for older children and adults about the environmental crisis created in collaboration with climate scientist Professor Ed Hawkins for Hay Festival.

petr Horáček

Petr Horáček was born in Czechoslovakia and grew up on the outskirts of Prague. From the age of 15-19 he studied at the High School of Art in Prague, which specialised mainly in design.

From age 19 Petr worked in a state design studio for two years, then studied painting at the Academy of Fine Art in Prague from 1988, graduating with a Master of Fine Art degree in 1994. As a student he met his English wife Claire and in 1995 they moved to England.

Petr started to write and illustrate books soon after his first child was born. The first of these, *Strawberries are Red* and *What is Black and White?*, were published in 2001, and he received the Books For Children Newcomer Award in the same year.

Since then Petr has written and illustrated many books for children, including a previous collaboration with Nicola Davies, *A First Book of Animals*, and has been translated into many languages, as well as winning awards for his books in Britain, the USA and Holland. More about his books and paintings can be found at www.petrhoracek.com.

Nicola Davies

Graffeg Books

For a complete list of titles by Nicola Davies
published by Graffeg please visit www.graffeg.com